WE HELP ONE ANOTHER

by
Alex Hall

Minneapolis, Minnesota

Credits
Images are courtesy of Shutterstock.com. With thanks to Getty Images, Adobe Stock, Thinkstock Photo, and iStockphoto. Cover – MNStudio, america365, Barks. 2–3 – wavebreakmedia, lilett, Polina Tomtosova. 4–5 – blvdone, Fotokostic, lilett, Rawpixel.com, alexdndz. 6–7 – FamVeld, Monkey Business Images, Polina Tomtosova. 8–9 – Jacob Lund, Volurol, FamVeld, Marina Zlochin, Polina Tomtosova. 10–11 – Pixel-Shot, Lopolo, lilett. 12–13 – Dmytro Zinkevych, LightField Studios, Ronald Caswell, fizkes, Polina Tomtosova, lilett. 14–15 – BearFotos, ESB Professional, Roberto, Polina Tomtosova. 16–17 – addkm, Gorodenkoff, Polina Tomtosova, lilett. 18–19 – M_Agency, wavebreakmedia, Alrika, Polina Tomtosova, lilett. 20–21 – Monkey Business Images, fizkes, Polina Tomtosova, lilett. 22–23 – wavebreakmedia, Tint Media, Polina Tomtosova, lilett. 24 – lilett, Polina Tomtosova.

Bearport Publishing Company Product Development Team
Publisher: Jen Jenson; Director of Product Development: Spencer Brinker; Editorial Director: Allison Juda; Editor: Cole Nelson; Editor: Tiana Tran; Production Editor: Naomi Reich; Art Director: Kim Jones; Designer: Kayla Eggert; Designer: Steve Scheluchin; Production Specialist: Owen Hamlin

Library of Congress Cataloging-in-Publication Data is available at www.loc.gov or upon request from the publisher.

ISBN: 979-8-89577-028-3 (hardcover)
ISBN: 979-8-89577-459-5 (paperback)
ISBN: 979-8-89577-145-7 (ebook)

© 2026 BookLife Publishing
This edition is published by arrangement with BookLife Publishing.

North American adaptations © 2026 Bearport Publishing Company. All rights reserved. No part of this publication may be reproduced in whole or in part, stored in any retrieval system, or transmitted in any form or by any means, electronic, mechanical, photocopying, recording, or otherwise, without written permission from the publisher. Bearport Publishing is a division of FlutterBee Education Group.

For more information, write to Bearport Publishing, 3500 American Blvd W, Suite 150, Bloomington, MN 55431.

CONTENTS

WE ARE CONNECTED 4
HELPING ONE ANOTHER 6
HELPFUL HEROES 8
TEACHING THE FUTURE 10
HELPING AT HOME 12
SPREADING KINDNESS 14
VOLUNTEERING 16
HELPING CHARITIES 18
ASKING FOR HELP 20
WHY IT IS GOOD TO HELP 22
GLOSSARY 24
INDEX 24

WE ARE CONNECTED

The world is full of people. We are all connected in a society. Together, we can make sure everyone has what they need.

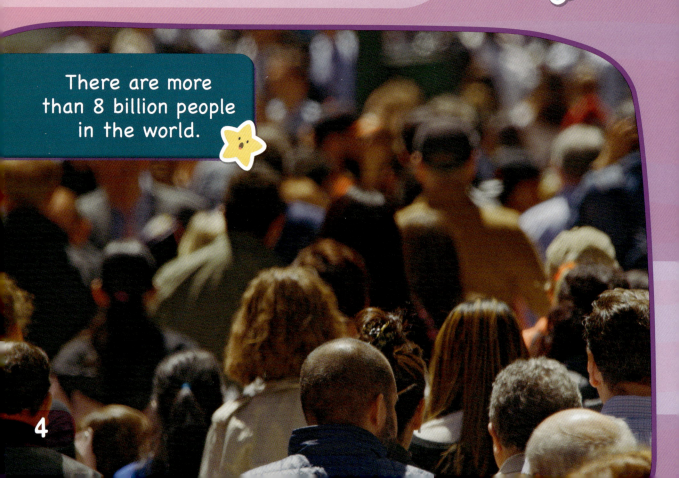

There are more than 8 billion people in the world.

What communities are you part of?

Within our society there are many different communities. These are groups that share things in common. Some communities are connected by a language or religion. There are also communities formed by people who all like the same thing, such as a sport.

HELPING ONE ANOTHER

We could all use a little help sometimes. Luckily, our communities are there to **support** us. We can be there for others when they need help, too.

When was the last time you needed help?

There are many ways to give and get help every day. Let's find out how we help one another.

HELPFUL HEROES

There are many helpers all around the community. Some people take care of others as part of their jobs. Police officers and firefighters work to keep everybody safe.

A FIREFIGHTER

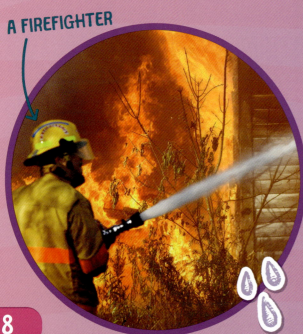

A POLICE OFFICER

Firefighters and police officers often take action during **emergencies**. These heroes are there for people on very hard days.

Doctors and nurses are heroes, too. They help people stay healthy. They also **treat** people who are sick so they can get better.

TEACHING THE FUTURE

How do these helpful heroes learn to do their jobs? Teachers help them gain the important skills they need. Some of these workers go to college. Many have on-the-job training.

Teachers at colleges are sometimes called professors.

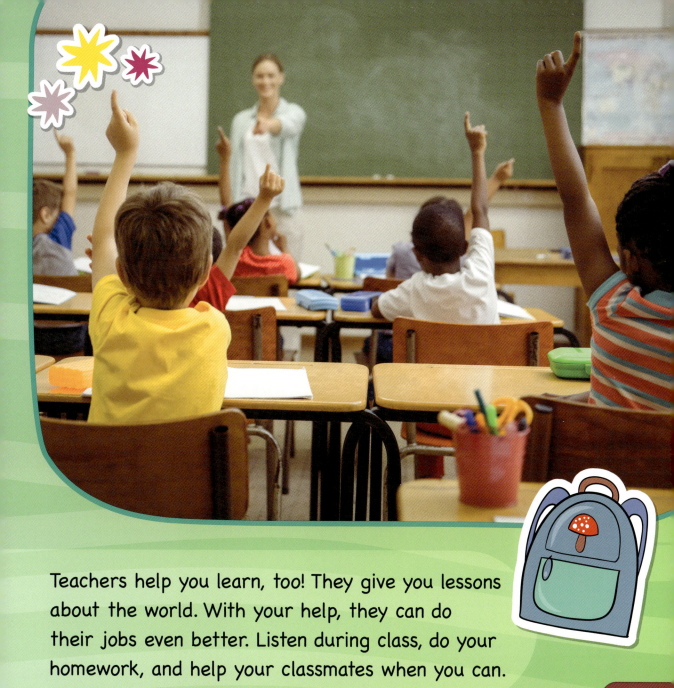

Teachers help you learn, too! They give you lessons about the world. With your help, they can do their jobs even better. Listen during class, do your homework, and help your classmates when you can.

HELPING AT HOME

Grown-ups at home often do many things for you. They might cook your food or clean your clothes. When you help out, you can learn a lot and have fun, too.

HOW COULD YOU HELP YOUR GROWN-UP?

One day, you will be a grown-up. You will have to do a lot for yourself.

Try setting or clearing the kitchen table. Fold and put away your own clothes. If you help your grown-ups, they may have more time to play with you!

SPREADING KINDNESS

Being kind is another big way to help at home and throughout the community. This makes sure everybody feels their best. Check in with your friends and family. Are they happy?

What could you do to help cheer someone up?

Holding the door for others is kind.

One act of kindness can **encourage** others to be kind, too. They may do something for someone else. Soon, everybody in the community may get the help they need.

VOLUNTEERING

Volunteering is when people give their time to help people without being paid. Many people volunteer at food banks. They feed people who are having a hard time getting food for themselves.

Some food banks cook warm meals for people.

16

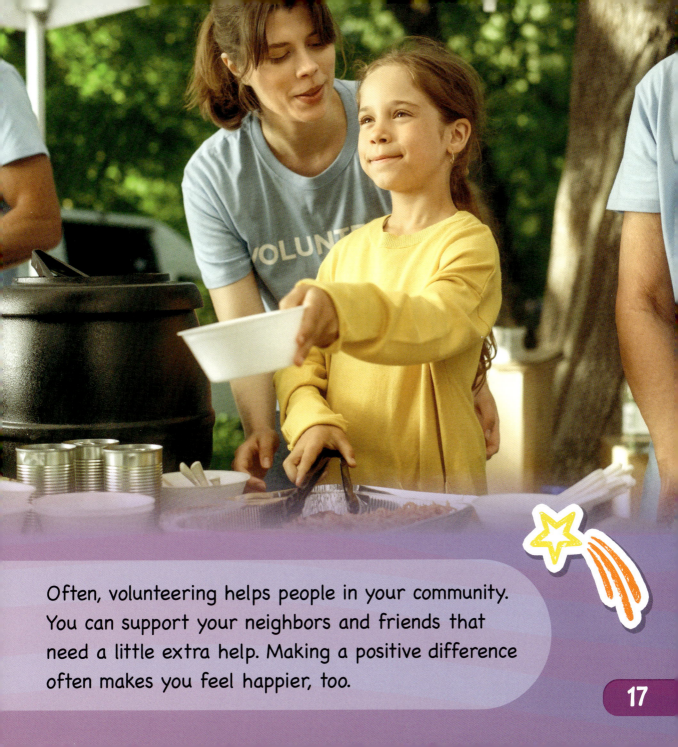

Often, volunteering helps people in your community. You can support your neighbors and friends that need a little extra help. Making a positive difference often makes you feel happier, too.

17

HELPING CHARITIES

If you do not have extra time, try giving to **charities**. These are groups that aid people or animals in need. Many charities collect **donations**.

Do you know about any charities in your community?

Things you no longer use or need could be given to help someone else.

People may donate toys or clothing to charities. Then, the charities can pass along these supplies. Most charities also take donations of money. This helps them do their important work.

19

ASKING FOR HELP

It is great to support others. It is also important to ask for help when you need it! Do you ever need help with your homework? Sometimes, we need to talk about something that makes us sad.

THINK OF A GROWN-UP YOU FEEL SAFE TALKING TO.

It can be hard to know how to ask for help. Try going to someone you trust. Your family, friends, or teachers may be able to help if you need it.

WHY IT IS GOOD TO HELP

There are so many ways to help one another. We can help grown-ups at home, volunteer, and donate to charities. When we support others, they will be there for us when we need it.

What kind of society do you want to live in?

Helping people makes them happy. It can give you happy feelings, too. This makes our society a nice place to be. It is better when we are all connected!

GLOSSARY

charities groups that raise money or take donations to help people, animals, or causes in a community

communities groups of people who live together or share things in common

donations gifts of money or supplies to help people in need

emergencies sudden or dangerous situations

encourage to inspire or support someone or something

support help and encouragement

treat to look after in order to help or fix someone

volunteering doing a job to help others without getting paid

INDEX

charities 18–19, 22

communities 5–6, 8, 14–15, 17

donations 18–19, 22

emergencies 8

grown-ups 12–13, 21–22

heroes 8–10

kindness 14–15

support 6, 17, 20, 22

teachers 10–11, 21

volunteering 16–17, 22

work 8, 19

24